Kings of the Forest

TREES

Kings of the Forest

ANDY HIRSCH

:01

First Second

New York

For the tree huggers

First Second

Copyright © 2018 by Andy Hirsch

Drawn in Clip Studio Paint EX. Colored in Adobe Photoshop CC. Lettered with Comicrazy font from Comicraft.

Published by First Second
First Second is an imprint of Roaring Brook Press,
a division of Holtzbrinck Publishing Holdings Limited Partnership
120 Broadway, New York, NY 10271
All rights reserved

Library of Congress Control Number: 2017946156

Paperback ISBN: 978-1-250-14310-5
Hardcover ISBN: 978-1-250-14311-2

Our books may be purchased in bulk for promotional, educational, or business use. Please
contact your local bookseller or the Macmillan Corporate and Premium Sales Department
at (800) 221-7945 ext. 5442 or by e-mail at MacmillanSpecialMarkets@macmillan.com.

First edition, 2018
Edited by Dave Roman
Book design by John Green
Trees consultant: Lewis J. Feldman

Printed in China by Toppan Leefung Printing Ltd., Dongguan City, Guangdong Province
Paperback: 10 9 8 7 6 5
Hardcover: 10 9 8 7 6 5 4 3 2

When most people think of trees, they don't picture a lot of action. Trees seem to be stuck in place, unaware of what's happening around them and unable to do much about it. This impression is completely wrong!

Even though plants have no eyes, they are very aware of the amount of light and the colors around them. They grow in the direction of more light and can tell the difference between green plants and other objects, like rocks. They can also anticipate when they are about to be shaded before it actually happens!

Even though plants have no mouths or tongues, they grow more roots in the places where soil contains the nutrients they want. And they can produce chemicals that make them more efficient at taking up those nutrients.

Even though plants have no noses, they can sense chemicals in the air that tell them when their neighbors are being attacked or eaten. They can then respond by ramping up their own defenses.

Even though plants have no ears, they can sense vibrations caused by feeding insects and then protect themselves.

Even though plants have no hands, they can interact with objects that they contact. This lets them grow around rocks or attach to useful structures if they are climbing vines.

All of these cool and sophisticated behaviors happen even though they have no brain.

This comic introduces you to some of the amazing things that trees can do. When I was a child, I first became fascinated with trees by making collections of leaves in the fall. I collected the most colorful leaves I could find and placed them to dry between pages in a big book. I was always disappointed that it was so hard to find perfect leaves—they all seemed to have a few holes in them. It made me wonder why almost all leaves had bites taken out of them but very few were eaten completely. Only years later, when I was officially working as a scientist, did I get interested in this observation again. The answer to this riddle seems to be that when an insect takes a bite out of a leaf, the tree responds by changing that leaf in many ways. Some of these changes make the leaf a less desirable meal for that insect. So the insect moves to another leaf that hasn't had a bite taken out of it yet. By the end of the season, almost every leaf has a bite or two missing. These changes are similar to an immune response by the tree.

There are still many things that we don't know about trees. For example, we don't know much about the language that trees use to communicate with one another. How do they understand that an insect is attacking their neighbor? Do all trees use a similar language? How do plants perceive chemicals in the air or vibrations in their shoots? How do they make decisions when there are conflicting signals?

Anyone can think like a scientist. It is not about knowing all the facts but more about being curious and allowing yourself to wonder, less about being an expert or a true believer and more about being open to the evidence. Your observations may provide us with the scientific breakthroughs of the future!

—Richard Karban,
professor of entomology, member of the
Center for Population Biology at the University of California, Davis,
and co-author of *How to Do Ecology: A Concise Handbook*

2

3

4

Different species of trees show different degrees of apical dominance.

A ponderosa pine grows straight as an arrow. None of the lower buds even think of challenging the lead.

Very bossy.

A crape myrtle has many trunks. They seem to lead by committee.

Oh, pretty!

Baobabs change their habits as they age.

Is this real?!

Cytokinin, a plant hormone like auxin, can free buds from dominance. Some tree diseases and pests cause out-of-control cytokinin production, resulting in what's called a *witch's broom!*

⇌Ulp!⇋

15

WHOOOOOOOAAA!!

Yes, both chloroplasts and mitochondria originated as independent organisms, meaning plants are symbiotic down to their very cells!

Wait, symbi-what now?

Symbiotic! Any organism that depends on another for survival is in a symbiotic relationship.

When *both benefit* from the arrangement, as the cells we just met do, their symbiosis is said to be *mutualistic.*

If one benefits and the other is *unaffected,* the relationship is *commensal.* Small epiphytes, plants that grow on plants, use trees' great height to get closer to the sun.

If one benefits from hurting the other, it is *parasitic.* Large epiphytes, like the strangler fig, harmfully squeeze their host while climbing them to steal their sunlight. How terribly rude.

The duration of light is the *photoperiod,* an essential signal for seasonal behavior like flowering and leaf fall.

More specifically, it is the period of *darkness.*

If a tree plans to flower in the spring, it is waiting for night to last *less* than a certain number of hours.

And if that same tree plans to drop its leaves in autumn, it is waiting for night to last *more* than a certain number of hours.

Were it able to combine the visual information from each leaf, a tree could have a surprisingly full view of its world!

37

38

39

42

46

A tree can fertilize its ovules with its own pollen, but it's healthier in the long run for different trees to reproduce with one another—that's *outcrossing*.

There're lotsa different conifers, an' each has its own way of *dispersin'* seeds far an' wide!

White pine seeds have *wings* that let the wind carry them long distances.

Sendin' offspring away from their parent trees means even if things get tough at home, the family line survives.

Lodgepole pinecones don't open 'til they've been *cooked* by forest fire, even if that means waitin' years an' years. Fires result in extra-nutritious soil for new seeds.

Pinyon pines have big ol' seeds that're picked up an' stashed by birds who'll fly 'em far away but'll likely forget where they hid *some* of 'em.

Knobcone pinecones stay on the branch after openin' to drop seeds. Eventually new wood can *grow over 'em!*

Juniper cones fuse an' turn *juicy.* They're easy to mistake for berries an' are a favorite of many animals.

If we're talkin' about help from other critters, though, we oughta talk about *angiosperms*, which include both eudicots an' monocots. *Hup!*

These trees reproduce using *flowers* that grow at their apical meristems. *Sepals* and *petals* make up the outside of the flower an' are often real colorful.

Inside you'll find male *stamen*. The *anther*, this bit on top, produces pollen—similar to male cones.

Pollen needs to find its way to the *stigma*, an' then to ovules made in the central *ovary*. *Carpels* are sets of female organs.

Flowers come in countless varieties, an' many lack one part or another. A common variant among trees is the *catkin*, a droopin' spike covered in lotsa tiny flowers.

For me?!

Unlike gymnosperms, which rely almost exclusively on wind to spread pollen, angiosperms work with lotsa critters, 'specially bugs and birds.

Why would, *uh*, critters want to pollinate flowers?

Oh, they don't really care about pollination—they're after *food!* Flowers attract pollinators with sweet, delicious nectar.

Sometimes pollen or even the flower itself is the treat!

Flowers can be specialized to attract certain pollinators. A white flower stands out to bees, one that only opens at night is prime for moths, an' large petals're perfect landing spots for butterflies.

Now, to get at that food, the pollinator'll have to get all up on the flower. If the flower has anthers, the pollinator'll get *covered* in, well, pollen!

When they look for more food at a different flower, they'll introduce pollen to stigma, an' there you go!

Flowers want pollinators to stick around, spreadin' as much pollen as they've got, so they treat 'em right, offerin' food, shelter, an' by raisin' their temperature, a warm place to spend the night!

zZZzz

Gymnosperms spend a lot of energy producin' pollen. Outta this sea of the stuff maybe *one* grain will stick.

Achoo!

ACHOO!

By redirectin' some energy to flower makin', angiosperms can *sniff!* make *much* more efficient use of pollen!

Ha-ha! This tree is a forest—an ecosystem all its own!

Every tree's an ecosystem! You've seen it: a tree absorbs sunlight to grow big an' tall...

...herbivores feed off the tree... carnivores eat the herbivores...

...birds an' mammals an' more shelter among branches an' roots...

...deadwood provides nutrients to fungi an' new plants...

...countless living beings may depend on a single tree for food an' shelter.

Wheee!

The most important detail about a tree's environment is its *latitude*, how far north or south of the equator it is. This determines how much sunlight is available.

Sunlight means *energy*, and it turns out energy is a good predictor of *species diversity*.

There are estimated to be **60,000** species of trees in the world!

Wow! That's almost 61,000!

At the North Pole, the *very highest* latitude, there aren't any trees, none at all.

Fly down to a *middle latitude* and things start to pick up, though. Nine species make up almost all of Canada's native trees.

By the time you make it to the equator, a *zero degree* latitude, you're likely to find hundreds or thousands of species per square kilometer!

That's nuts!

Another reason for all this species diversity is ice ages. When the Earth cools, glaciers and low temperatures wipe out high-latitude trees and split up tropical forests.

Now related trees are totally cut off from one another, cut off!

Over many generations, isolated populations can become their own *species*.

When the Earth warms, the forests reconnect and become a patchwork of extra-diverse areas!

High-latitude areas have to start from zero, all the way from zero, and only the hardiest tree species can cope with this less fertile environment.

Less diversity, just like we see today!

Trees are found in lots of different environments, and they have special adaptations for each. On the coastal edges of the tropics, you'll find *huge* mangrove swamps.

Are they growing in *salt water?*

Yes, indeed, yes. This environment has plenty of sun, nutrients, and water, but it's got plenty of harmful *salt* as well. That's why mangrove trees have an extra filtration layer around their xylem and some excrete salt from glands in their leaves.

These roots provide a safe, very safe breeding ground for all sorts of fish and crustaceans.

But don't roots need oxygen to respire?

Many mangroves have stilt roots like these, which start above the water. Others have snorkel roots that grow upward!

All are able to use the tide to help them, well, *breathe.*

Fresh air comes *iiin* with the low tide...

...and *ooout* with the high tide.

And what a variety of potentials there are! Hydra-like *yews* can grow multiple new trunks if one is lost.

The *dragon tree* has a distinctive umbrella shape and an even more distinctive *bloodred* resin.

Banyan seeds germinate on other trees and grow multiple trunks by dropping roots as they grow outward. Their crowns have been known to reach over 120 meters across.

Didiereaceae look like this. Can you believe they look like *this*?

Redwoods, the tallest of all, create the cool, wet climate they want by condensing enormous amounts of mineral-rich coastal fog in their leaves and drip-feeding the water down to their roots during the day.

They're the front line in the cycle of transpiration that builds clouds to move farther inland. Each successive tree keeps it going by passing water along.

It's not just trees that are important—it's *forests*. Without uninterrupted forest, the system breaks down.

—GLOSSARY—

Allelochemicals

Chemicals produced by plants for defensive purposes. These can be antibiotic, insecticidal, or otherwise unpleasant to eat.

Apical Dominance

The chemical inhibition of secondary growth by the lead shoot. Along with environmental factors, this determines what shape the tree's body takes.

Angiosperm

A category of tree also known as broadleaves or hardwoods. They reproduce through flowers, the ovaries of which enclose their seeds, and are often pollinated by animals.

Auxin

A growth-regulating chemical essential to plant growth. In different concentrations, it can encourage or impede growth in order to direct it.

Bark

The portion of secondary wood formed outward from the vascular cambium. It is divided by the cork cambium into phloem and cork.

Bud

An undeveloped leaf, flower, or shoot. These form at shoots' apical meristems and may remain dormant for long periods of time.

Compartmentalization

The process by which a tree seals off damaged areas of itself to prevent rot and infection.

Cone

The reproductive organ of a gymnosperm. Female cones are larger than males and will seal up after being pollinated.

Convergence

The evolutionary principle whereby unrelated species develop similar forms as a result of similar responses to their environment. The opposite principle applied to closely related species is divergence.

Cotyledon

A plant's first leaves enclosed within the seed. They hold the plant's initial food supply and do not last long after germination.

Deciduous

A type of tree that drops its leaves each year.

Flower

The reproductive organ of an angiosperm. For more details see page 65.

Fruit

The mature ovary of an angiosperm. It encourages seed dispersal and comes in many forms. For more details see pages 68 and 69.

Germination

The beginning of a plant's growth from a seed.

Gymnosperm

A category of tree also known as conifers or softwoods. They reproduce through cones, which hold their naked seeds and wind borne pollen.

Herbivore

An animal that eats plants.

Intelligence

The capacity for an organism to choose an action based on awareness of its environment and past experience.

—GLOSSARY CONTINUED—

Keystone species

A species essential for the survival of many others.

Leaf

A plant organ that grows from shoots and generally acts as the site of photosynthesis. Small openings called stomata allow for the intake of carbon dioxide.

Meristem

A tissue capable of producing any kind of plant cell. Apical meristems are found only at the ends of shoots and roots, and lateral meristems, the vascular and cork cambiums, are found within the length of the tree's limbs.

Monocot

A type of tree whose seeds contain only one cotyledon. They generally do not undergo secondary growth to create wood so may not be considered "true" trees.

Mycorrhizal network

The underground web that connects trees to one another. Formed by symbiotic relationships with fungi, it allows for the transfer of nutrients and chemical messages between individuals. It is the key to a healthy forest.

Periderm

The protective layer of bark formed outward from the cork cambium. It includes cork, which insulates the tree from pests, germs, and fire.

Phloem

A tissue formed outward from the vascular cambium that facilitates the movement of sugars down the tree for use and storage.

Photoperiod

The duration of darkness. Plants measure this to determine the season and schedule events such as flowering and leaf drop.

Photosynthesis

The process by which a plant combines carbon dioxide, water, and sunlight to form oxygen and digestible sugars. Its counterpart is respiration.

Plant cell

The basic unit of the plant surrounded by a cellulose cell wall. Cells contain many organelles, tissues, and pigments. For more details see pages 28 and 29.

Pollination

The process of tree fertilization. Pollen makes its way from a male cone or floral organ to a corresponding female. Trees are capable of self-pollination, when the same tree has both male and female organs, as well as outcrossing, when the organs are found on separate individuals.

Primary growth

Growth from apical meristems. This is how a plant gets longer and taller.

Respiration

The process by which a plant combines digestible sugars with oxygen to form carbon dioxide, water, and energy. Its counterpart is photosynthesis.

Root

A plant's typically underground limbs. They gather water, oxygen, and minerals while holding the plant in place.

Secondary growth

Growth from lateral meristems. This is how a tree gets thicker.

Seed

The protective container for a newly developing plant.

Shoots

A plant's stem, trunk, and branches. They are divided into nodes, where new leaves, flowers, and shoots develop, and internodes, where the shoot is focused on primary growth.

Spore

A tiny organism created between generations of trees. They produce the single-celled gametes that combine to form a seed.

Symbiosis

A relationship in which one organism depends on another for survival. Three types of symbiosis are mutualism, when both organisms benefit; commensalism, when one organism benefits with no effect on the other; and parasitism, when one organism benefits and the other is harmed.

Transpiration

The process by which water moves upward through a tree. Water taken in at the roots is pulled upward as a result of water evaporating from the leaves.

Tropism

Directional growth. This is how plants move their bodies in reaction to gravity (gravitropism), light (phototropism), and touch (thigmotropism).

Wood

A tissue resulting from secondary growth in trees. It allows for the movement of substances within trees and provides structural support. For more details see page 43.

Xylem

A tissue formed inward from the vascular cambium that facilitates the movement of water and nutrients up the tree. Old xylem becomes mineralized heartwood and functions as structural support.

That's a LOT of acorns!

The tallest redwood is **3,500** acorns tall!

The deepest fig tree's roots reach nearly **3,700** acorns down!

The heaviest jackfruit weighs more than **5,000** acorns!

The largest banyan tree's crown is more than **12,000** acorns around!

The biggest giant sequoia has a trunk volume of over **130,000,000** acorns!

The oldest bristlecone pine is **5,067** years old! You can't measure *that* in acorns!

Look! I'm life-sized!

For those with a calculator, Acorn is 33mm tall, 25mm across, and weighs 8g. That's a humble start for a mighty oak!

118

Pin oak

Red maple

Black willow

Paper birch

Sugar maple

Quaking aspen

—BIBLIOGRAPHY—

Books

Chamovitz, Daniel. *What a Plant Knows: A Field Guide to the Senses*. New York: Scientific American / Farrar, Straus and Giroux, 2012.

Raven, Peter H., et al. *Biology of Plants*. 8th ed. New York: W.H. Freeman and Company, 2013.

Tudge, Colin. *The Tree: A Natural History of What Trees Are, How They Live, and Why They Matter*. New York: Crown Publishers, 2005.

Wohlleben, Peter. *The Hidden Life of Trees: What They Feel, How They Communicate—Discoveries from a Secret World*. Translated by Jane Billinghurst. Vancouver: Greystone Books / David Suzuki Institute, 2016.

Other publications

Brown, Peter M. "OLDLIST." Rocky Mountain Tree-Ring Research. Web accessed August 8, 2017.

"General Sherman, the Biggest Tree in the World." Monumental Trees. Web accessed August 8, 2017.

Gorzelak, Monika A., et al. "Inter-plant Communication through Mycorrhizal Networks Mediates Complex Adaptive Behaviour in Plant Communities." *AoB Plants* 7 (2015).

Gumtow-Farrior, Daniel, and Catherine Gumtow-Farrior. "Wildlife on White Oaks Woodlands." Portland, OR: Woodland Fish and Wildlife Project, 1997.

Karban, Richard. "Plant Behaviour and Communication." *Ecology Letters* 11 (2008): 727–739.

Marosvölgyi, Marcell A., and Hans J. van Gorkom. "Cost and Color of Photosynthesis." *Photosynthetic Research* 103 (2010): 105–109.

Martin, Glen. "World's Tallest Tree, a Redwood, Confirmed." *SFGate*. September 29, 2006. Web accessed August 8, 2017.

Trewavas, Anthony. "Intelligence, Cognition, and Language of Green Plants." *Frontiers in Psychology* 7 (2016): 588.

Lectures

Feldman, Lewis J. "Plants and Fungi." Biology 1B, University of California, Berkeley, Berkeley, CA, spring 2015.

Moen, Gary. "Tree Biology: Their Structures and Their Functions." Boise Public Library, Boise, ID. Lecture, March 5, 2014.

Simmard, Suzanne. "How Trees Talk to Each Other." TEDSummit, Banff, AB, Canada, June 2016.